Being a Christian

by Fr Enzo Bianco

*All booklets are published thanks to the
generous support of the members of the
Catholic Truth Society*

CATHOLIC TRUTH SOCIETY
PUBLISHERS TO THE HOLY SEE

Contents

Introduction 3

I say I am a Christian - What does that mean? 4

1. Where does Christ fit into the world?...............6

2. What did his contemporaries make of Jesus?....9

3. What did Jesus say about God?......................12

4. What did Jesus say about people? 15

5. How was the 'mystery' of Jesus discovered? . 18

6. Am I one of the friends of Jesus too? 22

7. How did Jesus organise his friends?........ 26

8. The 'Our Father': prayer or blueprint? 30

9. Blessed are the poor or blessed
   are the cunning?..................... 33

10. The Sacraments: are they signs?
    And if so, of what? 37

11. The eucharist. Am I on the guest list too? ... 40

12. Forgiveness. Can we overcome evil? 43

13. Are we responsible for history? 46

14. Me and the Church:
    what is there for me to do?............. 49

15. According to Jesus,
    What does the future hold 52

Introduction: Being a Christian?
What on earth does it really mean?

This is the story of a typical ordinary person with a Christian background. A person whose life is OK enough, but whose faith has never developed beyond what he was taught in his confirmation classes. It is the story of his quest to discover what it really means to be a Christian and what Christ should mean to him.

I say I am a Christian
- What does that mean?

I have always assumed that I know what a Christian is, but when I look for words to explain it, I can't find them. Only then does it dawn on me that it's a question I really can't answer.

I was certainly baptised - that much I am sure of. Somewhere there is a font where a priest gave me my name a long time ago and added 'I baptize you'.

There is probably still a dusty old register in the parish archives where it is stated that on that distant day, with me still tiny and in nappies, accompanied by celebrating parents and relatives, I became a Christian without knowing it. But since then … have I lived as a Christian?

I'm not at all sure about this. It would be quite fair to say that I've been getting along all right without too many worries. To be honest, I suppose I'm not that good - but then I don't believe I'm that bad either. I'm a bit afraid that I'm really neither fish nor flesh. And here I am now, pondering this strange question: 'What does it mean to be a Christian?'

Recently I came across one of Pascal's famous 'Thoughts', and it struck a real chord: 'There are three kinds of people: those who have sought God and found him, and these are reasonable and happy;

those who seek God and have not yet found him, and these are reasonable and unhappy; and those who neither seek God nor find him, and these are unreasonable and unhappy.'

It might have been written for me.

On the face of it I seem to be happy enough: and yet deep down I know I'm not. I feel I ought to be looking for God. I want to understand, I want to be able to live a reasonable and happy life. My teachers taught me to ask questions, and now I'm asking: who is Christ? What is a Christian? In short, who am I?

I feel as though I already know the answer, an answer that was again suggested by Pascal. In another stunning 'thought' he imagined the Lord saying to him: 'Take heart': you would not be looking for me if you had not already found me'.

1. Where does Christ fit into the world?

Beginning my search for Christ, I look around me. I find so many signs of his presence - churches with bell-towers pointing up to the heavens, crosses.

Crosses on mountain peaks, in cemeteries, around people's necks. Footballers making the sign of the cross as they come onto the field. And I find the names of saints, those faithful imitators of Jesus, all over our maps, in our street names, on our signs.

Every seven days, on Sundays, believers gather in their millions in churches to meet with Christ in spirit, to listen to his message, and to receive the Lord Himself in the Eucharist as their spiritual food.

Every day, morning and evening, believers turn to him in prayer, in a dialogue where they find guidance for their life choices. I sometimes do that myself too.

An institution blazes a two-thousand year trail through time, it is a beacon and a guide for believers: it is called the Church. The popes point out the way to everyone, calling for a 'civilisation of love' to be realised in the world; and there are quite a few believers out there making it real.

It is also true that far too many of us believers live pretty mediocre and unimpressive lives, yet the presence and the work of some who are totally devoted to God and to their fellows - the saints - has in the long term had a profoundly improving effect on the levels of behaviour of humanity.

It's not that difficult to see that through his presence, his doctrine, and his followers, Christ has in fact influenced our way of thinking and living on this planet and has indeed changed our world.

As the *Catechism of the Catholic Church* tells us, history is a dramatic struggle between good and evil, but Christ lives in history and directs it towards the realisation of values of truth, freedom, community, peace and beauty.

I am perfectly aware that there are discordant voices. Down the centuries some have proclaimed the end of Christ. In 1773 Voltaire assured humanity:

'In the coming culture there will no future for the Christian superstition.'

In 1847 Ernest Renan prophesied: 'To me it is as clear as daylight that Christianity is dead, well and truly dead'.

In 1851 Pierre-Joseph Proudhon set another deadline: 'Christianity will be done for within twenty-five years'.

Later Nietzsche even proclaimed the death of God.

But in reality, modern thinking just can't get away from Christ. The celebrated nineteenth-century Idealist philosopher Benedetto Croce, despite denying any kind of transcendence, still felt obliged to write a note with the title 'Why we cannot not call ourselves Christians.'

It's hard to deny that the Christian faith has a huge internal dynamism which has given a real boost to humanity. So much so that it has been considered reasonable to divide history into two parts and make the coming of Jesus Christ the watershed between the years BC and AD.

They Said

With his pierced hand this being, the purest of the powerful and the most powerful of the pure, has knocked empires off their foundations and changed the course of the torrent of the centuries.
(*Johann Paul Richter*)

It is true that Christ appeared on earth but for a moment and in a remote and historically insignificant region, and yet in spite of that he remains the pivot and the apex of a universal maturing process.
(*Pierre Teilhard de Chardin*)

Jesus Christ does not belong just to Christianity, he belongs to the whole world. (*Mahatma Gandhi*)

The word of God

I want to think about these words of St Paul: God, when the fullness of time came, sent his son. (*Galatians 4:1-7*)

2. What did his contemporaries make of Jesus?

I am wondering what Christ's contemporaries made of him: their point of view seems crucial to me. And it's easy enough to check through the four Gospels and study their reactions in the context of the ways and customs of the time, which are well enough known nowadays.

His fellow-countrymen knew him as a Jew from a Jewish family, a carpenter in Nazareth. The son of a young woman from the area, a certain Mary, Jesus worked in the workshop with Joseph, who was assumed by all to be his father. In daily life he was a pious man, i.e. he kept religious observances and the Law of God. We know that he went on pilgrimage to the temple in Jerusalem.

We also know that he was definitely not a celebrity and that his trade would certainly never have brought him wealth or success.

The society in which he lived would not have been any better than ours. Palestine was occupied by Roman legions, people paid tax to a distant emperor. The leaders of the people steered a middle course to try and avoid the worst for their own people. But certain marginal groups were straining at the leash and plotting rebellion.

We know that one day Jesus left his family and began to preach as a wandering prophet. He showed sympathy for children, he was moved by the sick, he had gentle words of pardon for all, even for prostitutes and murderers.

In sum he sided passionately with the truth. John, one of his first disciples, records that he was devoted to the cause of truth: 'I came into the world for this, to bear witness to the truth; and all who are on the side of truth listen to my voice' (*John* 18:37).

Another of his disciples, Matthew, records that he insisted on sincerity: 'All you need say is 'yes' if you mean yes, 'no' if you mean no; anything more than this comes from the Evil One'. (*Matt* 5:37)

He had a generous and compelling idea of the moral life. Matthew again has passed down to us this general principle of his: 'Always treat others as you would like them to treat you' (*Matt* 7:12).

But more than by his words, Jesus taught by his way of life. For this we have the testimony of Peter, the disciple to whom Jesus gave special authority: 'Christ suffered for you and left an example for you to follow in his steps. He had done nothing wrong and had spoken no deceit. He was insulted and did not retaliate with insults; when he was suffering he made no threats but put his trust in the upright judge' (1 *Peter* 2:21-23).

He had the civil and religious authorities of his people against him, and in the end they made sure he was condemned to death.

10

His disciples, who described him so well for us, saw in Jesus a 'mystery' both unfathomable and disturbing; it motivated them to dedicate their lives to him, even to the point of laying down their lives for him, for they all died martyrs except one (John, who perhaps loved him more than the others).

I too feel the attraction of this crucial point of the 'mystery of Jesus'. I will push on with my quest, hoping to understand.

They Said

If Jesus Christ were to come today, people would not even crucify him. They would ask him to dinner, and hear what he had to say, and make fun of it. (Thomas Carlyle)

Attention! This man is extremely dangerous! His message of freedom and love is incendiary, it is a particular snare for the young ... This wandering preacher is still at large, and he constitutes an enormous danger for our consumer society.
(From the Hippy Manifesto, 1968)

The Word of God

Reflect on the radical humanity of Jesus Christ, rereading the passage where he claims that children must have the right to meet him and be close to him. (*Luke* 18:15-17)

3. What did Jesus say about God?

One day, says the gospel writer John 'The Pharisees sent the Temple Guards to arrest him … but no-one actually laid a hand on him. The guards went back to the chief priests who said to them: 'Why haven't you brought him?' The guards replied: 'no-one has ever spoken like this man'' (*John* 7:32, 44-46).

In this my quest for Jesus I must of necessity concern myself with what he said, for it was so powerful that those who heard him remained loyal to him in life and in death. Soldiers armed to the teeth did not lay a hand on him because they felt themselves subjugated and disarmed in his presence.

What did Jesus say about God?

God was - if I understand correctly - his favourite subject. However, he did not present God as the Supreme Being, the Abstract, Perfect, Omnipotent One, but as the good Father who loves us; as One who - like someone in love - takes care of those whom he loves and desires their good. One who calls men to himself, to take part in his own life, to share his happiness.

The term that Jesus used was father, but sometimes he used another more tender expression - we might even call it childlike. The children of Palestine used the Aramaic terms *imma* and *abba*, translatable as

Mummy and Daddy. Rather than the high-sounding words of the philosophers, Jesus preferred a child's language in speaking of God. The term *abba*, daddy, was for him the most appropriate way of expressing an absolute intimacy and the tenderness of God.

The *Catechism of the Catholic Church* tells us that we need to grasp that we are loved from eternity and called by name; that we are not on this earth for no reason, and that we are never alone either in life or in death. We can fail to love God, but we cannot prevent him from loving us first.

From the very earliest centuries of Christianity this conviction has come down to us, that God is a Daddy whose love for us is like a mother's. St Clement of Alexandria (among others) wrote: 'By his mysterious divinity, God is Father. But the tenderness he has for us makes him a mother. In loving, the Father becomes feminine'. In essence - as I found in the Catechism - God is 'the maternal father'.

As I understand it, God may be transcendent but he is certainly not distant. 'He is the highest yet the closest, he is the remotest yet the most present to us' (*St Augustine*).

Israel's history tells us that God went with his people on their journey and was intensely involved in what happened to them. He asked to be loved (the greatest commandment) 'with all your heart, with all your soul, with all your strength' (*Deut* 6:5). Sublime in his transcendence, he nonethless bent down to look with predilection at those lying in the depths of despair, in the dust, and even - to use the actual words of the psalmist - on the dungheap.

The way Jesus presents the Father to us is entirely different from our own mode of thinking. The Catechism tells us that he is both attentive and omnipotent, but not intrusive. He is close even when he seems to be absent. He does not prevent harm but draws good out of it, respecting the freedom of his creatures.

Having spent his whole life meditating on the words of the Lord, John, the disciple whom Jesus loved, came out with this stunning definition: 'God is love'.

They Said

For us Christians, believing means knowing that we are loved. (*François Mauriac*)

We want God to give us proof of his existence, but he only gives us proof of his love. (*Gilbert Cesbron*)

Do you want me to tell you something strange? When I became a father, I understood that God is father of all men. (*Honoré de Balzac*)

4. What did Jesus say about people?

This quest of mine to discover what life is all about, what Jesus Christ means to me, and what I am for him and for others, is becoming fascinating. I am looking through a book that makes sense, I am sifting through memories of my childhood faith, I am making space for new intuitions, I am finding truths that disturb me, they encourage me to keep on sifting. I've already been surprised by what Jesus said about God, now I want to find out what he said about us.

The first step - and a very obvious one - is that if God is our Father, then we are his children. God is first of all the Father of Jesus: in his baptism in the Jordan, this voice was heard: 'You are my son' (*Luke* 3:22).

God is also the father of the disciples of Jesus: in our baptism we become brothers and sisters of Jesus and children of the Son. John says we are 'called God's children, which is what we are!' (1 *John* 3:1). And Paul adds: 'if we are children, then we are heirs' (*Rom* 8:7).

The Father has put into each one of us a stupendous potential for life and he wants it to grow. He takes watchful care that everything - and that includes evil and pain - should work together for the good of his children.

The truth about our relationship with God and with others had already been etched by the prophets into the consciousness of the chosen people, and it was also the theme of the Covenant. But Jesus filled it out with new developments and brought it to full maturity.

Maturity at the level of the individual person, for Jesus soldered together the two greatest commandments which had appeared in the Old Testament separately: 'You must love the Lord your God with all your heart, with all your soul, and with all your mind. This is the greatest and the first commandment. The second resembles it: You must love your neighbour as yourself. On these two commandments hang the whole Law, and the Prophets too' (*Matt* 22:37-40).

On the level of the community of his friends, Jesus organised a society around Peter and his successors that had its base on earth and its summit in heaven: 'You are Peter, and on this rock I will build my Church' (*Matt* 16:18).

On the level of the whole of humanity, Jesus talked about the Kingdom of God, of which (and this one quotation will suffice) Georges Bernanos said: 'There isn't a kingdom of the living and a kingdom of the dead: there is the Kingdom of God, and we - living or dead - are all in it'.

Consequently the disciples of Christ turned to the Father with the attitude suggested by Jesus in the 'Our Father'. This is not a singular but a plural prayer, and with its seven requests it is much more than a prayer; it is a blueprint for living, a programme for individuals, for groups, and for humanity.

Moreover the disciples of Jesus accepted to live the Beatitudes as taught and practised for the first time by the Lord. At first sight the Beatitudes look disturbing and even dowright unacceptable, they seem shocking to the good sense of the man in the street. Nonetheless the true Christian lives by the Beatitudes.

For the person who accepts the perspective of Jesus, the appearance on the horizon of this new humanity represents a further step forward in cosmic evolution - one which Darwin with his materialism could neither foresee nor even imagine: after homo sapiens, homo mitis (the gentle man), who loves, and inspires the world to further progress.

They Said

The atheist is a son who tries to convince himself he has no father. (*Alphonse de Lamartine*)

The moment I believed there was a God, I understood that I could not do anything else but live for him. (*Charles de Foucauld*)

5. How was the 'mystery' of Jesus discovered?

'The beginning of the gospel about Jesus Christ, the Son of God'. As if to say: now I am going to tell you how the good news that Jesus is the Messiah and the Son of God began to be spread.

With these words Mark - the first gospel writer and the inventor of the literary genre called the gospel - opened his account of how the apostles came to discover the mystery of Jesus. That is, the mystery of a fascinating man who couldn't be pigeonholed and even looked like an extremist, because he was more than a man: the apostles and the disciples had to recognise (as Mark would tell everyone forty years after the event) that Jesus is God.

How did the apostles come to discover the mystery of Jesus? The evidence before them was substantial indeed.

There was his way of speaking, noted by the temple guards: 'No-one has ever spoken like this man' (*John* 7:46).

Matthew too remarked on it: 'his teaching made a deep impression on the people because he taught them with authority, unlike their own scribes' (*Matt* 7:28-29).

Moreover, the apostles observed that his words were so powerful that they actually produced miracles. Jesus addressed a command to the turbulent waters of the lake, and they subsided. He addressed commands to illnesses, and they gave way to health. He addressed commands to demons, and they fled. He summoned his friend Lazarus from the tomb, and Lazarus came out resurrected.

Furthermore, Jesus did not simply allow his divinity to be sensed, he actually declared it openly. In front of the apostles: 'Philip ... Anyone who has seen me has seen the Father, so how can you say, 'Show us the Father' Do you not believe that I am in the Father and the Father is in me?' (*John* 14:9-10).

And in front of the Jews: 'The Father and I are one.' The Jews understood perfectly well what he was saying, and they picked up stones to throw at him: 'We are stoning you ... for blasphemy; though you are only a man, you claim to be God' (*John* 10:30, 33).

He also foretold his own resurrection, and when this actually took place the apostles finally gave him their trust unreservedly. John concludes that in Jesus 'The Word became flesh, he lived among us' (*John* 1:14).

Here is a presence that changes the world. Jesus Christ reveals himself to the apostles as God's solution to the problem of evil - the overcoming of sin by mercy and forgiveness.

Jesus reveals Himself as God's solution to injustice and misery. Luke presents him to us as the liberator, as someone sent like the prophet Isaiah - but with a very different influence on history - 'to proclaim liberty to captives, sight to the blind, to let the oppressed go free' (*Luke* 4:18).

Ultimately, by his resurrection and the eternal life he offers in the kingdom, Jesus reveals himself to be the solution to the problem of death. Paul puts it like this: 'God raised up the Lord and He will raise us up too by His power' (1 *Cor* 6:4).

The greatest adventure of all is to discover the mystery of Jesus.

They Said

The empty tomb became the cradle of Christianity. (*St Jerome*)

The two worlds that had always been separate, the divine and the human, collided in Christ. A collision not through an explosion, but through an embrace. (*Sören Kierkegaard*)

The surname of Jesus was God. (*An entry in an anthology of children's sayings edited by Tullio De Mauro*)

Jesus is God with skin on. (*A little girl in a catechism class*)

Jesus Christ is a God to whom we draw near without pride, and before whom we lower ourselves without desperation. (*Blaise Pascal*)

In the tomb I will find the cradle. (*Giacomo Zanella*)

20

Reflect on the mystery of Jesus as received by the apostles, rereading the prologue to the Gospel of John. (1:1-18).

6. Am I one of the friends of Jesus too?

Continuing my quest, I am going to check out how Jesus gathered disciples around him from the start and developed a network of intense personal friendships.

His friends were ordinary people, especially fishermen. Some he invited to follow him more closely, and they left their families. He said to them: 'Come after me and I will make you into fishers of people' (*Mark* 1:17). There was also a certain Matthew, a tax collector, a collaborator in the pay of the Roman authorities. Jesus said to him too: 'Follow me' (*Matt* 9:9) and he devoted himself to the new cause. There were also some women in the group.

From among these special friends Jesus chose twelve more trusted men whom he called apostles - from a Greek word meaning 'for mission'. Twelve like the tribes of Israel, because they were called to form the new people of God. So now Jesus had by his side a whole group that went with him everywhere, resolute and courageous.

Being with Jesus transformed them. They discovered - and it was the fisherman Peter who acknowledged it - that he had 'the words of eternal life' (*John* 6:68). Gradually Jesus devoted less and less time to the crowds and more and more time to training these special friends of his. He encouraged them with amazing promises: 'There is no need to be afraid, little flock, for it has pleased your Father to give you the Kingdom' (*Luke* 12:32).

After the death and resurrection of the Lord they devoted every moment of their lives to telling everyone about Jesus, and they died martyrs, i.e. witnesses.

Eventually other friends, seeing that death was taking its toll of these first fundamental witnesses, hurried to set their stories down in writing, to prevent them from being lost for ever: and so it was that the four gospels came into being. With the addition of some letters written earlier or later and some other writings, the New Testament was born.

My impression is that through all his earthly life Jesus continued to offer his friendship to all those around him; and it doesn't really matter that those years are now so long ago, because deep down I too feel that I am being called to become his friend here and now.

I am also realising that this new emotional attachment has no effect on the externals of my existence, my commitment to my work or my involvement in my family alongside the folk I love so deeply. But inside I am changing. All this happens to me and to so many others the moment we opt to be real Christians, i.e. real friends of the Lord.

Down the centuries, Jesus has continued to welcome these friends of his into that social reality on earth which from the very start he entrusted to Peter: 'On this rock I will build my Church' (*Matt* 16:18).

The Church, the people of God - the person who becomes a friend of Jesus becomes a part of it. Friendship with him makes us all friends of each other. And we feel the presence of the one who said: 'Where two or three meet in my name, I am there among them' (*Matt* 18:20).

They Said

If you want to be young again, treat Jesus Christ as your contemporary. (*Tonino Bello*)

Christ was the radiant companion of my childhood and adolescence, and now and always he is the radiant companion of my family and professional life. (*Louis de Funès, comedian*)

The day that you no longer burn with love for Christ, many will die of cold. (*François Mauriac*)

It is a beautiful and gracious thing to care passionately about the Messiah. (*Jacopone da Todi*)

Jesus is a wound from which you do not recover. (*Ibn Arabi*)

Reflect on the betrayal of friendship: in Judas (*Matt* 26:14-16, 47-50) with a tragic outcome (*Matt* 27:3-10)

...and in Peter (*Matt* 26:31-35, 69-75) with forgiveness and a renewed trust (*John* 21:15-17)

7. How did Jesus organise his friends?

Pondering what I have already learnt, I note that this new life in Christ is not a life for solitaries, it is a life in the family; and the family of the children of God is the Church. 'Church', a word of Greek origin, signifies 'assembly': the church is the great family assembled by Christ.

The Book of Acts tells us that after the Ascension of Jesus to heaven, the friends he had gathered around him continued to live together. 'These remained faithful to the teaching of the apostles, to the brotherhood, to the breaking of bread and to the prayers. ... And all who shared the faith owned everything in common. ... The whole group of believers was united, heart and soul ... None of their members was ever in want.' (*Acts* 2:42, 4:4, 32:4).

Christians are very deeply united, they live out the mystery of communion in Christ. He prophesied this: 'And when I am lifted up from the earth, I shall draw all people to myself' (*John* 12:32).

Another image: 'I am the vine, you are the branches' (*John* 15:5).

Paul suggests a further image in the Letter to the Ephesians: Christ is the Head (vital directive principle) and the Church is like the body, the living extension of him.

Paul soon became aware of this union between Christ and Christians - indeed he lived it personally in the celebrated dialogue on the road to Damascus: "Saul, Saul, why are you persecuting me?' 'Who are you Lord?' ... 'I am Jesus, whom you are persecuting' (*Acts* 9:4-5).

Persecution of Christians is here shown to cause personal wounds to Christ.

The Church is a community of faith, hope and charity. The theological virtues have the dynamism to unify Christians in the flow of time. They are bound together by their faith in the Word of Jesus, they remind each other of it. They find fulfilment in fraternal love, as Jesus taught them. And they live in hope of the gradual fulfilment of the Kingdom of the heavens promised by the Lord.

And there is more. Christians know that Jesus did not come only for them. At the moment of leaving them, he said 'Go into all the world, preach the gospel and baptise all peoples' (*Matt* 28:19). This means that the Church is not a closed group, it is open and dynamic and orientated towards others. Christians know that the greatest gift they can give is to share their faith, they are well aware that they are missionaries.

So much for the theory, but is it really always so in practice? Unfortunately not, for the truth is that we Christians usually do not feel very responsible for the Church. We think responsibility is a matter for the Pope, for the bishops, or for the priests and the sisters. It's not a matter for the likes of us, it's not a matter for ordinary believers. And yet the truth is that all of us are Church and I too have my personal responsibilities, I too have my place and my mission. I cannot behave as though I was unemployed…

Frankly, when I decided to figure out just what Jesus Christ meant for me, I did not imagine that finding the answer could cost me so much. Now I understand the observation of Guillaume Pouget that 'Christ is not found because he makes us too uncomfortable'.

They said

In the vessel of the Church we are all part of the crew, there is nobody who is a passenger.
(*Yves Congar*)

When I think of myself on my own, I feel like a worm; but when I consider myself as member of the Church, I feel huge: a sharer in the intelligence of Augustine and Thomas, in the art of Fra Angelico.
(*G.K. Chesterton*)

Praise be for ever to the majestic grandmother, on whose knee I learnt everything! (*Paul Claudel*)

We want to make the Church so beautiful that everyone will fall in love with her and want to come in. (*John XXIII*)

Never tire of reading the story of the Early Church in Acts chapters 1-2.

8. The 'Our Father': prayer or blueprint?

The gospel writers tell us that the Lord often went off away from the group of disciples and walked up into the hills to find a place to pray on his own. The apostles, as good Israelites, must have valued prayer; but as they spent time with Jesus and were able to observe him, they realised that his praying was different. They wanted to learn it. They said: 'Lord, teach us to pray'. Then Jesus replied: 'When you pray, this is what to say ...' (*Luke* 11:1-2). And so we have the 'Our Father'.

In the Gospels there are two versions of the text: *Matthew* 6:9-13 and *Luke* 11:2-4. The first is more or less the one we use today. But I find that the 'Our Father' is much more than a prayer. It doesn't just say to the Father, 'Intervene, do this or that'. It binds the person who prays to look at things from the point of view of the Father, and to ask to be associated with him as a protagonist in fulfilling his plan for humanity and for the world.

The first word in this prayer is 'Father'. Actually Jesus said Abba, an Aramaic word suggestive of tenderness as in a child's talk: Daddy. This is the great revelation that Jesus gave us about God, and since then 'Daddy' has become the new definitive face of God for us.

After 'Father', we add the adjective 'our'. Not 'my' but 'our'. Not 'give me' but 'give us'. We pray in the plural 'Forgive us …, deliver us from evil'. Not on our own, each one for himself, but in a group, in community. And so we emerge from our isolation, from our solitude. At home it is the family that prays, in church it is the community.

What do we pray for? First of all 'May your name be held holy (hallowed)'. But …. Isn't the Father the very source of holiness, the 'thrice holy? Does he need us to declare him holy? The reason for this petition is that his holiness - which ought to be shining out in the world in all its splendour - is clouded by the sin of us believers. The Church, to be credible, must be holy.

Then Jesus wants us to ask for help so that we can feel we are brothers and sisters committed to the implementation of a renewed society, called to form the Kingdom of God. So he makes us ask: 'your kingdom come'. The Church is committed to a project which transcends her: although she begins the task here on earth it will be completed only in a future dimension in God.

Then we ask for inspiration to put into practice the blueprint of the kingdom: 'your will be done'. It is not a despotic and capricious will: it is the will of God, therefore reasonable and good, motivated by fatherly feelings, with absolute respect for the freedom of his children.

What we are definitely not meant to do is to start by praying to be relieved from our three or four little daily bugbears or infirmities; instead we pray for that great reality, the kingdom, the community of persons united to Christ.

Jesus, who has his heart in heaven, shows he has his feet on earth. So he invites us to transform everyday situations and the common needs of life with our prayers.

he invites us to ask for bread. Not my bread, but our bread: not each one for himself, but all for all.

He calls us to an attitude of mutual comprehension: we are to ask for the Lord's forgiveness, but only to the extent that we feel ourselves ready to forgive others.

He enjoins us to call for help in moments of weakness, when temptation can make us slip into sin.

The 'Our Father' is like a compendium of the whole Gospel. Indeed it seems to me that it has such explosive power that it can eliminate an entire category of persons: orphans.

They said

Chew over the 'Our Father' the way you do with liquorice: then you'll get all the sweetness out of it. (St Bernardine of Siena)

9. Blessed are the poor or blessed are the cunning?

Two opposite things strike me about Jesus: the strongly spiritual dimension of his teaching, which is consistently marked by the highest idealism.

A down-to-earth commitment to the concrete situations of our daily life, without illusions as to our evil and sin.

Jesus Christ is for ever the Word spoken by the Father from all eternity, the Word who has become incarnate in the flow of time, who reads the flawed heart of man like a book - for the simple reason that he created him.

At the start of his Sermon on the Mount, Jesus describes concrete life situations in which the freedom of men is at stake and calls on the disciples to stay with the logic of the kingdom of heaven up to its ultimate conclusion.

The Sermon on the Mount opens solemnly with the proclamation of the eight Beatitudes. Blessed are the poor in spirit, the suffering, the meek, those who hunger and thirst for justice, those who show pity, the pure in heart, the peacemakers and those who work for justice. Along with the proclamation goes a promise of happiness: they are blessed, because the Kingdom of Heaven belongs to them.

It is a logic that is utterly opposed to the logic of common sense, the logic of so-called good sense. What our normal instincts tell us is to say is:

Not blessed are the poor but blessed are the rich.

Blessed are those who laugh and have a good time.

Blessed are the cheats who get away with it.

Blessed are the bullies.

Blessed are those who expect 'everything now'.

Blessed are the victorious warmongers.

Blessed are the violent and the persecutors of the innocent.

These beatitudes are so familiar! And the results are visible to everyone: organised crime, corruption, exploitation, wars. But Jesus simply turned them all upside down.

Above all the Lord lived his Beatitudes and he lived them consistently right up to death on a cross. He is not one of those who make themselves invulnerable to suffering and run away from pain, and it was precisely by his consistency that he became credible.

In the Beatitudes Jesus proposes an attitude of detachment, generosity, commitment and devotion. But he does not call us to renunciation or passivity; rather, he calls us to a constructive presence in the midst of others, he calls us to be actors and protagonists.

What happens to people who live like this? Jesus promised them the kingdom. They 'will be comforted, they will be satisfied, they will find pity, they will inherit the earth, they will see God, they will be called children of God'.

Those who live like this imitate Jesus who is the example of true life, the divine model of the new humanity. We humans are intelligent because God is the highest intelligence. We are able to will because God is will and omnipotence. We love because God is love. We are free because God is supreme freedom. We are capable of giving because God is gift and absolute gratuitousness.

We will be welcome in the house of the Father to the extent that we become children who resemble their Father.

But ... it is within our power to follow those other beatitudes: blessed are the cheats, the rich, the bullies etc. And it happens. Freedom leads people into disorders, inconsistency, contradictions, delirium, and the madness of sin. Mark Twain said: 'Man is the only animal that blushes. Or needs to.'

And the Father respects our freedom. But in Jesus he has given us the model and in the Beatitudes the principles, the manifesto, the manual. For two thousand years he has been waiting for us to live as his children.

They Said

Blessed are who can laugh at themselves: they will always have something to amuse them. (*Anonymous*)

10. The Sacraments: are they signs? And if so, of what?

In my personal quest to find out what a Christian is, I come to the sacraments: a vast world of the spirit where I make entirely unexpected and quite fascinating discoveries.

At the bottom of everything I find a common experience. There are important realities of our inner world that we can express only by signs. Nobody will ever see the love that I feel for a person, I must express it to that person in a smile, a caress, a flower. And in the Church too - the height of spiritual reality - we must communicate by signs.

By the will and the plan of Jesus the Church is at once highly spiritual and heavily earthy. I live my concrete belonging to its spiritual dimension through very solid things that are visible and tangible: buildings for worship, seats of organisations, furnishings and sacred objects, parish registers, crucifixes ... My time is divided up according to the liturgical year, Sundays and feast days, morning and evening prayers, planned moments of reflection ... We meet, we communicate, we decide, we do concrete things.

Among so many gestures I find special signs that were willed by Christ from the beginning and called sacraments. These rites, evolved by the Church, are gifts from Jesus to his friends, gifts that introduce us to the life of faith and associate us with the divine plan of salvation.

They are signs that produce what they signify: grace (friendship with God and others), the will to live in love, the hope of an existence in God beyond death. There are seven of them: baptism, confirmation, the eucharist, reconciliation, anointing of the sick, orders and matrimony. For centuries, Christians incorporated this list into their morning prayers. Not that the list as such was a prayer, but going through it every day helped to recall them to the mind as essential rites of our Christian life.

As signs, the sacraments are formed of two inseparable elements, like the two sides of a leaf: they are made of one thing that refers to another thing.

For example, the gospels throw a flood of light on the sacrament of reconciliation. One day they presented to Jesus a paralytic for him to heal. The response of Jesus was to say: 'Your sins are forgiven you'. Faced with the stupor of those present, he went on: 'So that you may know that the Son of Man has power on earth to forgive sins, I tell you: get up, take up your bed and go home'. These are the two sides of the sacrament: the material, physical, visible side (the act of getting up and walking: semiologists would call it the signifier), the unseen spiritual aspect (the signified), the forgiveness of sins, the recovery of friendship with God.

Jesus chose poor things: a little water, a piece of bread, a sip of wine, a drop of oil, and he chose common actions: washing, eating and drinking, anointing. These may be earthy things but they point us to enormously important values in the world of the spirit.

In essence the sacraments are personal actions of the risen Jesus: he uses the Church both to proclaim salvation to humanity and to transmit to us the new life of the children of God.

Clearly the first great sacrament of salvation is Jesus Christ himself, who prolongs his action in the world through the Church, which is both a sign and an instrument of salvation.

They Said

The outer bulwark of the Church is stiff and bristling with moral teachings; but on the inside human life is dancing the way children do. (*G K Chesterton*)

The Word of God

Go back to the episode where Jesus gives proof of the forgiveness of the paralytic by healing his body. (*Matt 9:1-8*)

11. The eucharist.
Am I on the guest list too?

Continuing my quest for the Lord, last Sunday I went to mass. On the way I thought to myself: at this same moment millions and millions of people all over the world are going to church just like me, to meet Christ.

I imagined a map of the world, with its various time zones, the Sunday masses in the morning or evening or the vigil masses. Individuals or families in their Sunday best. And then the homilies of the priests explaining the Word of God to them, then the words of consecration and the processions of the faithful to receive the white Hosts.

I imagined the daily masses involving Christians in all kinds of communities, from monastic communities to school children in their chapels. Every day, in the most remote corners of the earth, for two thousand years and right down to the present moment.

From the time when the words of the Lord 'Do this in memory of me' were taken seriously.

This is how it all started. The apostles were used to having meals with their master in an atmosphere of friendship and serenity. Then came the one that was to be so dramatically called the 'Last Supper', the farewell banquet. Jesus took a loaf, he broke it and he gave it to the apostles, speaking mysterious words: 'Take it and eat. ... This is my body'. Then he took a cup of wine and gave it to them: 'Drink from this, all of you' (*Matt* 26:26-28).

Then came the words 'Do this in memory of me'.

After his resurrection the disciples remembered these words and took to gathering at table to celebrate the risen one together. It was a meal that turned into a rite.

From its most significant gesture, the rite became known in the Latin world as the breaking of bread, *fractio panis*. But the Greek term *Eucharistia* was also used, i.e. giving thanks, which is the term we now use for the sacrament. With this rite the Father is thanked for the gift of his Son, for his friendship, for salvation in his kingdom. But ultimately the term that stuck was the curious word *Missa* (Mass), which signifies sending: Christians are sent by Christ into the world to carry his message.

The Second Vatican Council summarised the place of the mass like this: 'The Church makes the Eucharist, and the Eucharist makes the Church'.

The Church makes the Eucharist, i.e. she celebrates the rite through the successors of the apostles - the bishops and the priests. But equally the Eucharist makes the Church. In other words it is capable of transforming Christians who feed on it, and it does this in very many ways.

We come to church to free ourselves from the torment of material things: we put our heads in our hands and go into silence and reflection before God.

The rite leads us to think about our sins and disorders. In a moment of truth we confess the evil we have done, we ask for forgiveness from God and from each other. Mothers, fathers, children, friends, neighbours…

Then we put ourselves in listening mode: through the Gospels Jesus talks to us too like he did to the crowds in Palestine. We discover our situation as children of God, loved in Christ, invited to live consistent lives. We renew our life plans.

Then Communion, an encounter with Christ in mystery, 'face to face with him'. We leave our places not each on his own account, but all together, like a people on a journey.

Then 'the mass is over', we return to our homes, and we take out into our lives what God has brought to maturity in us.

So it is that the Eucharist makes the Church.

They Said

If people knew the value of the Eucharist, the police would have to be called in to control the crowds at the church doors. (*St Thérèse of Lisieux*)

The mass is long when devotion is short. (*Proverb*)

12. Forgiveness. Can we overcome evil?

In trying to understand what a Christian is I have discovered the comforting presence of Christ; in the world, in time and in my own life. But I also find another presence that is equally invasive: the presence of evil. Both physical evil as expressed in physical pain and moral evil, a presence that is even more uncomfortable and worrying. In the confessional we call it sin.

I find evil everywhere where a choice is made for the easy comfortable life of selfishness. Injustices done to gain some advantage. Cheats and thieves, spouses unfaithful to their mutual love. Hatred, dishonesty and indifference. These are the squalid realities of everyday life.

Sin disrupts two relationships: first of all, our relationships with others. The person who sins refuses to live in fraternal love and makes himself and his own comfort the supreme goal of his life.

But sin also disrupts our relationship with God. This was all too well known to the holy King David, who, having committed adultery and then having made himself instigator of the murder of a servant of the state, expressed his penitence very clearly: 'Have mercy on me, God … Against you, you alone have I sinned' (*Psalm* 51:1, 4).

For Christians a sin always disrupts their friendship with Christ, a friendship which never diminishes, not even when Judas betrayed him with a kiss. For he calls even Judas 'Friend' (*Matt* 25:50) and tries to get him to look at himself: 'Are you betraying the Son of Man with a kiss?' (*Luke* 22:48).

But the love of Jesus is stronger than the sin of men. In the episode of the healed paralytic, he showed that he has power to forgive sins. They even heard him say: 'I came to call, not the upright, but sinners' (*Matt* 9:13).

To the adulterous woman he saves from stoning he says very simply 'Go away, and from this moment sin no more' (*John* 8:11). To the good thief crucified with him, he promises 'Today you will be with me in paradise' (*Luke* 23:43).

Looking at our hands stained with guilt, we could all too easily be assailed with an anxious fear, but John, the apostle whom Jesus loved, has already reassured us in his name: 'Even if our own feelings condemn us, … God is greater than our feelings and knows all things' (1 *John* 3:20).

Jesus, who forgave sinners he met during his public life, gave to his Church the sacrament of mercy, a rite that is a festival - the festival of forgiveness. Here the Church, the community of believers, becomes the place of liberation from evil and the place of hope.

Then Jesus in his turn wants his friends to be capable of forgiving. He does not want vendettas nor the infinitely precise justice of an 'eye for an eye' which transforms the earth into a kingdom of moles, into a world of the blind. He wants the mercy that he preached by his own example: 'Learn from me, for I am gentle and humble in heart' (*Matt* 11:29).

Darwin did not foresee it, but the new humanity, fruit of the evolutionary leap caused on earth by the incarnation of the Word, is formed not of the aggressive but of those who are gentle and humble of heart - and thus capable of forgiveness.

And so in the school of Christ the Church becomes an unexpected community of the forgiven who forgive.

They Said

When you are saying the Our Father, put in the name of the person who has upset you: "Forgive us our sins, as I forgive x". (*Norman Vincent Peale*)

Forgiveness cannot change the past, but it expands the future. (*Stanislaw Boros*)

Forgive quickly: you will save precious time, and you will have a better digestion. (*Cardinal O'Connell*)

Always forgive your enemies: nothing infuriates them more. (*Oscar Wilde*)

13. Are we responsible for history?

I push on with my quest: are we Christians responsible for history? Am I too responsible for my little life? What can I do? I begin to notice that the aimless drifting of my life has transformed into a purposeful journey.

The history of matter

Astronomers talk about a Big Bang or huge initial explosion more or less 15 billion years ago which is at the origins of matter, energy, space and time. In the first billions of years the world was made up of a few tiny elements: hydrogen, oxygen, traces of lithium. Then the List of Elements began to grow gradually until it reached its present count of 107 Chemical Elements.

Matter and energy, expanding into space, gave their origins to stars, constellations, galaxies and shoals of galaxies - including our Milky Way, a galaxy with 200 billion stars. Among them is the sun, 4.5 billion years old, and father of new planets, including the Earth (4.4 billion years old) and the piece of land on which my little home stands.

The history of life

Life began on earth 3.8 billion years ago. Out of a primordial soup the first single cell organisms were formed. Then, 700 million years ago, pluricellular organisms, vegetable and animal. Last of all 'mankind' finally made its appearance.

The history of humanity

The emergence of hominids goes back four or five million years; in the order *Australopithecus*, *homo habilis*, *erectus*, *neanderthalis*, *sapiens*, ... Finally *homo sapiens sapiens*, which could also mean 'man who knows that he knows'. Ten thousand years ago his first primitive working tools appeared and the first urban settlements. There are scholars who wonder about the *anthropic principle*. i.e. did evolution have a direction or a meaning? Is what has happened in the universe directed towards mankind?

Many scientists are not of this opinion, holding that man was born by chance and constrained to egoism and bullying in order to assert himself in the cosmos. Some have hypothesised the 'selfish gene' as the basis of evolution. They do not find dignity in humanity nor the greatness of the child of God.

The story of the children of God

In the Bible the believer finds truths about mankind which are exciting. Man is made by God and so resembles him. 'Let us make man in our own image, in the likeness of ourselves' (*Gen* 1:26).

So he is at the summit of creation: 'You have made him little less than a god, you have crowned him with glory and beauty, made him lord of the works of your hands'. (*Ps* 8)

And he has a special mission: 'God took the man and settled him in the garden of Eden, to cultivate it and take care of it'.

What does it mean to have the care of the earth? Teilhard de Chardin would say: so that it can be 'ready for the parousia'. That is: ready for the return of Christ at the end of time.

Humankind is a people on the way, but the way is not haphazard. God follows the events of our lives with love: he entrusted his promises to the people chosen by him. And 'when the completion of the time came, God sent his Son' (*Gal* 4:4) to fulfil these promises in the Word made flesh. To fulfil them in the Church, that mystical and earthly reality of which I too am a part.

God is in our history. But he does not impose himself on us, he does not go over our heads. He asks us to enter into his plan as protagonists and leaves us with our responsibility.

They Said

Man was not created to take orders from God, but to be a creator alongside him: to be responsible therefore for all that happens, and even for what doesn't happen. (*Maurina Zenta*)

14. Me and the Church: what is there for me to do?

So we are responsible for our own history. What will I do as a Christian in the Church? There is such a crowd of people pushing explanations at me: the Pope, the theologians, the parish priests, perhaps even the politicians... I prefer to be told by the Lord. One day he told the 'parable of universal judgement': 'When the Son of Man comes in his glory ... then he will take his seat on the throne of glory. All nations will be assembled before him... Then the King will say to those on his right hand, 'Come, you whom my Father has blessed, take as your heritage the kingdom prepared for you since the foundation of the world. For I was hungry, and you gave me food, I was thirsty and you gave me drink, I was a stranger and you made me welcome, lacking clothes and you clothed me, sick and you visited me, in prison and you came to see me'.

There are the works of mercy. The first Christians called them *opera Christi*, 'works of Christ', because he was the first to do them: 'Jesus went about doing good and curing all' (*Acts* 10:38). And they made them their 'code for living'.

There were six works of mercy: but in their eyes the number six was imperfect, and so for the sake of perfection they added a seventh: 'burying the dead'.

But these works involved only corporal mercy, and the Christians knew that man is made up of soul as well as body. So they added the seven spiritual works of mercy: counselling the doubtful, instructing the ignorant, admonishing sinners, consoling the afflicted, forgiving offences, suffering difficult persons patiently, praying to God for the living and the dead.

Christ's message to us includes these works of mercy. The sages of the first centuries and the Middle Ages selected them and explained them. They still retain their relevance even today and even for me.

But now, with the new problems arising from a society evolving with overwhelming speed, morality is getting very complicated. Ethicists are obliged to constantly define new and fascinating scenarios for the Christian conscience.

There is the urgent need for peace, of which so many people - often led by ambitious and brainless politicians and military men - are sadly deprived. But there are also small-scale wars, between social classes, between areas, between families. And at least on this very basic level, I too am called - to be a worker for peace.

A peace that postulates social justice. Respect for the rights of the worker, of the unemployed, of minorities, of immigrants. There is unlimited scope here for us Christians.

Our world is becoming smaller, a consequence of the phenomenon of globalisation: it is irreversible, but if it is not controlled it turns into a dangerous disaster. The Church, which condemned communism, condemns economic liberalism too when it places its laws above human persons. In one of their documents the Bishops of Holland spoke ironically of 'the freedom of the wolf in the free chicken coop'. The results of liberty when poorly-understood were already foreseen by Bishop Helder Camara, who spoke of the Third World countries as being 'in the process of underdevelopment'.

There are problems relating to the environment and to respect for nature. Waste, irrational consumption, with catastrophic consequences like the hole in the ozone layer, and the changes resulting from the greenhouse effect. These also depend on me, on how I use aerosols and the water out of the tap …

They Said

The Christian is a man to whom God has entrusted all men. (*St John Chrysostom*)

Jesus Christ frightens the world especially through the poor whom he represents. (*Primo Mazzolari*)

The Word of God

The parable of Jesus in *Matt* 25:31-46.

15. According to Jesus, what does the future hold?

There is an important aspect of life where I feel I need to question Jesus Christ in depth: death. Every so often someone we love dies and our bereavement feels like a dramatic separation, a wrong suffered, an injustice. And as to my own death, I don't even want to think about it, I feel as though I am made for life, for immortal life.

So then where does death come in?

As usual, the reply of Jesus wrongfoots us. In a discussion with the Sadducees, who denied immortality, he roundly declared that God 'is not the God of the dead but of the living' (*Matt* 22:32). God is not on the side of death but of life, and in Christ Jesus he overcame our death. Rising again, Jesus defeated it.

Now the Christian who entrusts himself to Christ knows that death is not the ultimate but only the penultimate thing. It is only a gateway to definitive life in God. God will be 'God-with-them. He will wipe away all tears from their eyes; there will be no more death, and no more mourning or sadness or pain. The world of the past has gone' (*Revelation* 21:3-4).

Studying the evidence of the Bible, Christian thinkers constructed a new science, called in Greek eschatology. That is, the science of the ultimate things, of the four last things: death, judgement, hell, paradise. This science tells us that beyond death life awaits us; that our loved ones who died in faith are alive in Christ. That this will be so for us too.

Death need not frighten us. St Therese of Lisieux (who died aged 24) said: 'I am not going to die, I am going into life… It is not death that is coming to fetch me, but the good God'.

In this Christian perspective, the judgement of God does not make us afraid. The other Teresa, Teresa of Avila, said: 'I am not afraid of the judgement, because the judge is my friend'.

Hell is born from the fact that man can always say to God: 'May your will not be done'. Then it is not God who condemns but it is rather man who excludes himself by his own choices. 'Hell', said Bernanos, 'is not loving any more'. As for paradise, God opens the door to all: anyone who wants can enter.

If and when we reach it, we may be in for some surprises. For example, how strange that we don't find certain individuals there whom everyone considered to be saints? On the other hand: good grief! How on earth did those suspect types get in? Finally: wow! I'm here too!

Jesus promised something of the kind to the apostles: 'I am going now to prepare a place for you' (John 14:2).

So what does the future hold for us? According to Jesus, the future is … Jesus.

I have loved life to seek God; now I love the death that will take me to him. (*Augustin Cauchy - Mathematician*)

Death is made so that we don't die again.
(*Antonin Sertillanges*)

He makes things too low who makes them under the stars. (*Thomas Young*)

If we kept on looking up at heaven, we would eventually acquire wings. (*Gustave Flaubert*)

The past is a broken egg, the future is an egg waiting to hatch. (*Paul Eluard*)

Waiting for the ultimate things implies a commitment to the penultimate. (*Dietrich Bonhoeffer*)

What we are is the gift God gave us. What we become is the gift we give to God. (*André Maurois*)

A Christian can be at peace as long as he is not too much at ease. (*Julien Green*)